Admissions to Independent Elite Boarding & Day Schools and Oxbridge & St. Andrews in the United Kingdom

Charlotte Courtenay

Copyright © 2024 by – Charlotte Elizabeth Courtenay – All Rights Reserved.

It is not legal to reproduce, duplicate, or transmit any part of this document in either electronic means or printed format. Recording of this publication is strictly prohibited.

Toll Free Calls: (US & Canada) 1-855-54-Elite (1-855-543-5483)
International Callers: 1-412-92-Elite (1-412-923-5483)

Email: Info@BoardingSchoolsIvyLeagueOxbridge.com

Table of Contents

Dedication	i
Acknowledgment	ii
About the Author	iii
Foreword	1
UK Elite Boarding Schools and the Relationship Relevance to Oxbridge and St. Andrews, and to other Elite Russell Group Colleges in Competitive University Admissions	2
Where to Begin	6
Summer Enrichment Pre-College Programs for Academically Gifted and Talented Youth	11
Things to consider when choosing a Boarding School and Pre-College Programs	12
Bonus: How to Get the Best Letters of Recommendation – Guaranteed!	16
How students should go about the business of obtaining the Best Letters of Recommendation/Expert Testimony:	16
There are two additional Primary Factors in the Admission Applications Process for Students applying to Graduate School or Professional School.	18
Bonus: Ace the Interview! Get Your Ivy League and or other Elite Prestigious College and University Offer!	18
A Final Note on the Admissions Process	21
Recommended Reading	26
Annual Calendar/Weekly Planner	27

Dedication

This First Edition of Admissions to Independent Elite Boarding & Day Schools and Oxbridge & St. Andrews in the United Kingdom is dedicated to:

Our British Monarch King Charles III and our entire Royal Family, Members of all Three Branches of Government who are Graduates of Boarding Schools, Oxbridge and St. Andrews, and other Elite Prestigious Russell Group Universities and Military Service Academies in our UK, including Ivy League and Stanford and MIT and other prestigious colleges and universities in the USA.

My parents, Mary & James, my siblings, Bernard & Samantha.

The Sisters of St. Joseph De Cluny Nuns, world headquarters in Paris, France.

In the memory of my late husband Raymond Jr. Genius IQ 185 to 205 range. He encouraged me to write this book. Raymond sustained a traumatic brain injury in a traffic accident. He died of Covid 19 in 2021 during the worldwide pandemic.

In the memory of late world leaders:

Her Majesty Queen Elizabeth II

His Majesty Prince Philip Duke of Edinburgh

British Prime Minister Baroness Dame Margaret Thatcher

Acknowledgment

My sincerest appreciation and gratitude to my dearest beloved father-in-law, Professor of Medicine Dr. G.A. Howard, for his encouragement and unwavering support in all my endeavors.

The conceptual framework for this admissions guidebook was written while I was a Graduate Student at the University of Oxford, England, in the United Kingdom. Then updated while working as a Deputy Warden in the largest Hall of Residence as well as Head of House named for the President, to Undergraduate and Graduate Students and Fellows at the University of St. Andrews, Scotland, in the United Kingdom. The framework updated again during a year post graduate research on Harvard campus in Cambridge Massachusetts.

This book was written during my time researching various types of Boarding Schools in the United Kingdom such as the 'Seven Original Public Schools,' and in the United States of America namely the 'The Eight Schools,' among other elite prestigious schools which collectively – historically are the 'Feeder Schools' to Oxbridge & St. Andrews and Ivy League & Stanford & MIT, other elect Russell Group Universities in the UK and other Prestigious Universities in the USA, including Military Service Academies in the UK & USA.

Many thanks to Project Manager Mr. James D., Account Manager Mr. Ryan H., Mr. Steve P., and the Editorial Team, the Book Cover Design Team, and the entire Team at Amazon Book Publications.

About the Author

The University of Oxford-Educated Social Scientist, Charlotte Courtenay, a New Times Best Seller, the sole proprietor of the International Consulting Company http://www.boardingschoolsivyleagueoxbridge.com, a Senior Education Consultant facilitating admission to top independent boarding and day schools and universities in the UK & USA, the most influential Political Strategist of our 21st Century, achieving political victories in elections for new and incumbent candidates for UK Prime Ministers, US Presidents and Vice Presidents, including the appointments of Cabinet Members and Supreme Court Justice Nominees, both Chambers of Congress, State Governors, G20 and OECD Heads of State, Heads of Multi-National Organizations, such as the Head of the UN and EU, G20 and leaders in countries and organizations such as the World Bank and IMF, University Chancellors & Presidents at institutions in our UK & USA and other leaders in countries and organizations around our world.

Foreword

In the United Kingdom and United States, about 10% of all children 5-18 years attend independent schools, including 1% in the UK and 1% in the US attending boarding schools, yet in both countries, 50% to 60% of all students at Oxbridge and St Andrews, Ivy League Stanford and MIT, attended independent schools in general, elite prestigious boarding schools in particular. This means 90% of all the children in the United Kingdom and United States are competing for only 40% to 50% of the admission spots available at Oxbridge and St. Andrews, Ivy League and Stanford and MIT. Students with aspirations of holding the highest offices of power - such as Prime Minister of the UK, Members of Parliament, President of the US, Members of Congress, Supreme Court Justices, Heads of Countries and International Organizations, Ambassadors, Heads of Financial Sectors, Head of Corporations, Heads of Hospitals, Heads of International Legal Firms, Heads of elite prestigious schools, colleges, and universities, must have as a prerequisite one or more degrees from Oxbridge or Ivy League. In most instances persons holding these positions are also a product of boarding schools.

UK Elite Boarding Schools and the Relationship Relevance to Oxbridge and St. Andrews, and to other Elite Russell Group Colleges in Competitive University Admissions

Parents and young adult students alike, engage in the decision whether to choose boarding school, local independent day school, or local state school. The consideration in the biggest why to select boarding school: which ones are worth considering, the primary reason the overwhelming number of families make this crucial decision – the boarding school option.

There's indeed a formula to gaining admission to Oxbridge and St. Andrews, and other elite prestigious Russell Group Universities in the United Kingdom as well as Military Service Academies, and in the US to Ivy League, Stanford and MIT. Admission to this distinguished club does not happen by chance, this takes years of appropriate preparation, brilliant strategies, and effective planning.

Charlotte, on behalf of the Courtenay Company, known as Boarding Schools Ivy League and Oxbridge, prepared this document specifically for parents and students embarking on the best decision to move ahead with the boarding school option. This is a guidebook thus included herein are links to the best boarding school options to gain admission to Oxbridge and St. Andrews in particular and other elite highly selective Russell Group Colleges and Universities in general. This document is not meant to be a complete list of all boarding school options in the United Kingdom. However, quick links to web addresses are provided to view more complete lists of independent schools. Indeed, the reason for putting forward this document is that parents and students have a step-by-step reference that is very concise to help families save valuable time and financial resources to navigate the boarding school search with competence and confidence, without employing others to complete the search for significant fees.

Let me get to the point. There are feeder pipelines from Junior Boarding Preparatory Schools to Senior Secondary Boarding High Schools, feeder schools to Oxbridge and St. Andrews and other highly selective elite Russell Group Universities in the United Kingdom. Gaining admission/membership into these most prestigious boarding schools is the guarantee of admission to Oxbridge and St. Andrews and other prestigious elite Russell Group Universities such as London Imperial College and Bristol, and the University of Edinburgh and Glasglow in the United Kingdom. All the wealthy families in this country have legacies at our most prestigious Independent Public-Boarding Schools, Oxbridge & St. Andrews and other prestigious elite Russell Group Universities. Indeed, over 50% of students past and present at Oxbridge & St. Andrews and the most prestigious colleges and universities are the product of independent schools. Although currently there are about ten percent of students in the country attending private schools, there are the original seven Independent Public-Schools - the most prestigious senior boarding schools (fee paying private schools, not to be confused with State Schools - non-fee-paying schools). These seven schools have an advantage to gaining admission to Oxbridge and St. Andrews and other elite prestigious Russell Group colleges and universities. Institutions of Higher Learning, consider students at Independent Public Boarding Schools much more prepared to be successful at top research universities.

Preparation for life begins prior to our birth. Parents who are graduates of an elite boarding school or a graduate of Oxbridge or St. Andrews or other elite prestigious Russell Group college or university; you may already know and understand how to navigate your children through this process. The aims and purpose of this book are that we at Boarding Schools, Ivy League and Oxbridge, want parents with or without a college/university diploma/degree, regardless of their financial resources, to read and understand this short guidebook framed with simplified language to help you with the process to elite boarding school admissions and subsequently elite college and university admissions. We want to create wider access to elite boarding schools for all students, thus creating wider access to Oxbridge and St. Andrews, and other elite prestigious Russell Group colleges and universities.

Do you intend to enroll your children in Junior/Preparatory Boarding School starting in Year 2 at age 7 years or Year 3 at age 8 years in the UK? Parents wishing to send children to Junior Boarding/Middle School (Year/Grade 6 at age 11 years through Year/Grade 8 at age 14 years) you need to start contacting and communicating with Admission Officers several years in advance of your children's enrollment.

Parents wishing to send their children to Junior and Senior Boarding Schools in the USA to prepare for admissions to Ivy League and other elite universities, can purchase our USA version guidebook by Caroline Courtenay on Admissions to Elite Boarding Schools and Ivy League in the United States of America.

To start reviewing options for Junior Boarding Schools in the United States which accepts children at Year/Grade 5 age 10 through Year/Grade 8 age 15 years. Senior Boarding Secondary High Schools in the UK accepts students from Year/Grade 9 age 13 years through age 18 years, Year/Grade 13 Lower Sixth Form age 16 years through Upper Sixth Form age 18 years (Year/Grade 11th & 12th in the USA context). In the USA, Senior Boarding Secondary High Schools accepts students from Year/Grade 9 age 14 years through Year/Grade 12 age 18 years and Gap Year/Postgraduates Year/Grade 13 age 18-19 years.

Parents need to plan carefully where they will raise their children from pre-preparatory ages 2 to 6 years old, as well as evaluate the quality of schools available locally – private independent schools and state schools. Are there excellent private primary school options for ages 2 to 6 years old? Are there high-quality state primary Grammar School options for Nursery and Reception from ages 2 years up to the age 11 plus year old students, Common Entrance Examination Academic and Exhibition Scholarships for Music and Sports at age 13 years?

Here's how to help your children gain admission to the elite boarding schools – of their choice – those highest on the League Tables, which will guarantee their admission to Oxbridge and St. Andrews and or other elite prestigious Russell Group colleges and universities.

Where to Begin

The Independent Schools Association website (ISA) can help you find Independent Day and Boarding Schools for your children. Pre-Prep Nursery Reception, Junior Preparatory Day Schools, Junior Preparatory Boarding Schools, Senior Secondary Day Schools, Senior Secondary Boarding Schools, Sixth Form College Day Schools, Sixth Form College Boarding Schools.

Please view the quick link to ISA https://www.isaschools.org.uk

List of UK Boarding Schools by categories here
https://www.boardingedu.com/country/boarding-schools-in-uk

The Independent Schools Council UK https://www.isc.co.uk

Also, see the list of Headmasters and Headmistresses Conference Schools: https://www.hmc.org.uk

First, select the best private school option for your children ages 2 or 3 years old to age 6 or 7 years old or ages 8 or 9 years old (depending on the age at which you wish to have your children start attending Junior/Preparatory Boarding School) in your local or nearby community or nationally League Table ranked school. Get to know the names of the top three private schools in your County or Parish or Borough. Visit each school with your child at age 2 or 3 years old, then make your final decision to apply for admission. Consider the values, interests, and needs of your children in particular, your family as a whole in general. Then, select the best choice for your children.

Toward the end of Reception or Year 1, Year 2 or Year 3, depending on the age at which you wish to have your children start attending Junior/Preparatory Boarding School. Have your children spend a couple of weeks during Spring break, summer programs at your top two or three final choices. Then apply to those schools in the autumn when your children are in Reception or Year 1 or Year 2 or Year 3 to start Junior/Preparatory Boarding School at the latest in Year 4 for solid preparation for the 11+ Examination or the more competitive Common Entrance Examination at age 13. Children have a 50 to 70% chance of admission acceptance rate to Junior/Preparatory Boarding Schools, which are the feeder pipeline schools for achieving matriculation to the most highly selective Senior Boarding Independent Public Schools. To start taking a look to learn more about these schools for admission to Junior/Preparatory Boarding Schools for children in Year 1 to Year 6, please refer to the Independent Association of Preparatory Schools in the United Kingdom. Here's the website: https://iaps.uk

Junior Day and Preparatory Boarding Schools do an excellent job in preparing students for the 11+ Examinations, as well as the Common Entrance Examinations at age 13, for admissions to Senior Day and the highly selective Boarding Independent Public Secondary/Schools. In contrast, waiting to start the boarding school admission process late in the game, until your children are ready to enter Year 9, at age 13 years, will put you at a disadvantage for successful application to the highly selective Senior Secondary Boarding Schools, where applicants in general have only a 12 to 25% chance of admission to the top most prestigious boarding schools including the Seven Original Senior Boarding Public Independent Schools which were all boys – today two are co-educational and several others admit girls in Sixth Form – Lower Sixth Form is Year 12 age 16 to 17 years, and Upper Sixth Form is Year 13 age 17 to 18 years (Grades 11 & 12 in the US context). To start reviewing competitive and prestigious Senior Secondary Boarding Schools in the UK – here are web addresses to those with the most successful applications to Oxbridge and St. Andrews and other highly selective Russell Group Colleges and Universities. They are the Public Schools primarily located in Southern England in general, Southeast England in particular, and several others in Scotland and Wales.

https://en.wikipedia.org/wiki/Public_Schools_Act_1868

See also lists of top Boarding Senior Schools in the UK, which include several all-girls and co-educational schools.

https://en.wikipedia.org/wiki/Category:Boarding_schools_in_England

https://en.wikipedia.org/wiki/Category:Boarding_schools_in_Scotland

https://en.wikipedia.org/wiki/Category:Boarding_schools_in_Wales

https://en.wikipedia.org/wiki/Category:Boarding_schools_in_Northern_Ireland

https://en.wikipedia.org/wiki/Category:Catholic_boarding_schools_in_England_and_Scotland

Attendance of these world renowned elite senior boarding schools almost always guarantee that in due course at graduation pupils will gain admission to Oxbridge and St. Andrews and other most elite, highly selective, prestigious Russell Group colleges and universities, or further afield in the other European Countries or Ivy League in the USA or universities in Asia, and in other home countries of the international pupils. As aforementioned, over half of all the pupils at these elite higher education institutions are the product of independent day and boarding schools; although about 10% of all pupils in the UK attend independent schools, and of that number only 1% attended boarding schools. In the United States, slightly fewer children of the percentage of all school-age children in the general population attend independent/private schools around 9%, and of that number, almost 1% attend boarding schools.

Indeed, all pupils at these elite boarding schools gain entry to Oxbridge and St. Andrews and or other elite, highly prestigious Russell Group Colleges and Universities in the United Kingdom, as well as to Ivy League and Stanford and MIT and/or elite, highly prestigious colleges and universities in the United States.

Senior Boarding Schools in the United Kingdom are as highly selective as Oxbridge and other elite, highly selective, prestigious Russell Group Colleges and Universities. The competition for a limited number of available places is very keen with so many applicants from the Senior Secondary Boarding Schools in the United Kingdom and from students in independent day schools and students in state schools across the United Kingdom, as well as students from overseas particularly from Europe and Asia. Get ahead of the competition by getting your children admitted to the feeder pipeline Junior/Preparatory Boarding Schools in the first instance for guaranteed acceptance to a top Senior Boarding Schools – the feeder pipeline schools to Oxbridge and St. Andrews and other elite prestigious Russell Group Colleges and Universities.

To start reviewing the top seven most competitive and prestigious Senior Boarding Preparatory Schools in the UK – here's the quick link to the Public Schools Act:

https://en.wikipedia.org/wiki/Public_Schools_Act_1868

Senior Boarding Schools do an excellent job in preparing students with rigorous courses to take the GCSE at the end of Fifth Form/Year

11 and A-Levels at the end of Year 13/Upper Sixth Form for admissions to Oxbridge and other elite, highly selective, prestigious Russell Group Colleges and Universities. To review a broader list of Junior Preparatory Boarding Schools which start at Year 2 to Year 8 (some end at Year 6), and Senior Secondary Boarding Schools which start at Year 9 (some start at Year 7) through Year 13/Upper Sixth Form, in some instances Year 2 to Year 13 for all-through boarding schools (these are not as the specialized Junior/Preparatory Boarding Schools, or the Senior Secondary Boarding Schools). All-through schools are primarily interested in keeping children at their schools from Reception age 5 years through Year 13 at age 18 years. The most elite prestigious Junior/Preparatory Boarding Schools and Senior Secondary Boarding Schools are overwhelmingly located in Southeast England in particular. Please refer to the list of oldest schools in the UK.

Please refer to the list of oldest schools in the UK.
https://en.wikipedia.org/wiki/List_of_the_oldest_schools_in_the_United_Kingdom

Boarding Schools, in general, in all parts of the United Kingdom are considered relatively very good.

Please refer to the comprehensive list of boarding schools in the UK via this link:
https://en.wikipedia.org/wiki/List_of_boarding_schools_in_the_United_Kingdom

Summer Enrichment Pre-College Programs for Academically Gifted and Talented Youth

Most Junior Preparatory Boarding Schools and almost all Senior Secondary Boarding Schools offer summer programs open to the general public, including to students from overseas.

https://en.wikipedia.org/wiki/List_of_the_oldest_schools_in_the_United_Kingdom

https://en.wikipedia.org/wiki/List_of_boarding_schools_in_the_United_Kingdom.

Also, consider summer programs at Junior Boarding Schools and Senior Secondary Boarding Schools in the US – refer to Admission to Boarding Schools and Ivy League for more details, as well as summer programs at Boarding Schools in Switzerland.

University of Oxford Summer School: Pre-University, Undergraduates, and Graduates. https://www.conted.ox.ac.uk/about/summer-schools

University of Cambridge Summer School: Pre-University, Undergraduates, and Graduates. https://www.ice.cam.ac.uk

University of St. Andrews Summer School: Pre-University, Undergraduates, Graduates:

https://www.academiccourses.com/universities/United-Kingdom/University-of-St-Andrews-International-Summer- Programmes

University of London – Imperial College
https://www.imperial.ac.uk

Things to consider when choosing a Boarding School and Pre-College Programs

History of the Institution – Read the founding history, including the list of Notable Alumni. Who's at the table? Former Notable Alumni as well as current students who will in the future chart courses of their own and no doubt will someday be added to the list of Notable Alumni. Notable Alumni whom you have never met are present at the table at all these institutions. Their achievements are also your shared history and legacy. Becoming a member of a world-renowned prestigious institution, you have membership in the same club of notables. Like members of our world-renown secret societies.

Review the list of The World's Most Elite Boarding Schools to select the best schools in the UK, US, and Switzerland.

List of G20 Schools:

https://en.wikipedia.org/wiki/G20_Schools

Resources – such as Cadre. What is the Education Level of the Faculty? What schools and colleges and universities they've attended. The number of volumes in the Library/Media Center, Computer Labs, Science Labs, and other Learning Centers. Campus Museums and Observatories.

Endowment size of the Institution – for the sustainability of the school/college or university as well as for Financial Aid for current and future students. Is admission 'Need-Blind,' are students admitted based solely on academic merit and talents without regard to their ability to pay fees? Or are students admitted solely on their ability to pay fees? The latter are not the best options for your family regardless of your financial circumstances.

Matriculation Destinations of Schools Leavers at Senior Boarding Schools to Oxbridge and St. Andrews and other prestigious Russell Group Colleges and Universities. The best indicator of Senior Secondary Boarding Schools reputation among Oxbridge and other elite prestigious Russell Group Colleges and Universities.

Elite Club Membership. When you arrive at Oxbridge, St Andrews, or other prestigious Russell Group College or University, you're already a member of an elite club – your particular boarding school; and having attended boarding school in general.

Proximity to others with Power and Wealth. Students make and build good network connections with others for Professional Networking prior to, during, and after college or university. The adage who you know is as important as what you know, rings true for graduates of these elite institutions. The Elite Club Boarding School Graduates, Oxbridge and St. Andrews, and other Russell Group Elite Prestigious Colleges/Universities are pervasive in our Country, especially in London – in all Three Branches of Government, on Downing Street, Westminster Parliament – House of Lords and House of Commons, the Supreme Court, and indeed in London's Financial District. When interviewing for dream career roles, chances are – the panel will likely be made up of graduates from elite Public Boarding and Day Schools, Oxbridge and St. Andrews, and other Russell Group Elite Prestigious Colleges and Universities, including Military Service Academy like Sandhurst.

List of Prime Ministers of the United Kingdom by Education

https://en.wikipedia.org/wiki/List_of_Prime_Ministers_of_the_United_Kingdom_by_education

Parents who decide to keep their school age children close to home at Prestigious Private Day schools or quality State Grammar Schools, Prestigious State Boarding Schools for the highly gifted students demonstrating the most academic promise can supplement their children's education in selecting a wealth of summer programs to help develop your children's academic curiosity, gifts and talents at Junior Preparatory Boarding Schools, Senior Secondary Boarding High Schools and at Universities offering Pre-College and Pre-University Programs. It is important to note that most of the State Schools on the League Tables are located in Southeast England, London in particular. Day School Pupils in Primary/Preparatory School Year 2 at age 7 years to Year 6 at age 11 years or to Year 8 at age 13 years, can choose Boarding Schools as a Summer Enrichment (see website lists of schools above.)

Parents should focus on their children's areas of interest or on areas where their children need more developmental support – English and other Modern Languages, STEM – Science, Technology, Engineering and Mathematics. Music – there are great options in London and Vienna to improve their skills on their instruments as well as The Julliard School https://www.julliard.edu in New York USA. Academic Year Abroad or Summer specialty study activities and opportunities, such as Pilot Training only 1:15hr to the field trip venues in Washington DC at Randoph Macon Academy in Front Royal Virginia https://www.rma.edu America's only full time High-School Flight Program, where students in Grade 6-12 starting at age 11 years, learn to fly airplanes before they learn to drive cars!

Athletics – Equestrian activities, improve their Golf or Tennis at the US top Sports Academy in the World https://www.imgacademy.com/boarding-school

Day School Pupils at Independent Public Schools or at State Comprehensive High Schools, Year 7 at age 11+ years or Year 9 at age 13 years through Sixth Form – Year 13 at age 18 years, can choose Boarding Schools as a Summer Enrichment (see web site lists of schools above), Oxbridge and St. Andrews and other elite prestigious Russell Group Colleges and Universities as a Pre-College Summer Enrichment (see web site lists of schools above) or conduct a wider search for other colleges and universities with Pre-College Programs.

Students take summer courses in residence at Senior Boarding Schools, Ivy League and other elite prestigious Colleges and Universities in the US can obtain our USA version guidebook on Admissions to Independent Elite Boarding & Day Schools and Ivy League & Stanford and MIT in the United States of America.

Enrollment in summer enrichment programs at Senior Boarding Schools, Oxbridge, Ivy League, and Switzerland, help students to gain experience with more rigorous college-level courses at prestigious institutions of higher learning with highly academically competitive, and motivated like-minded peers, in preparing for the highly selective college/university admissions process.

Bonus: How to Get the Best Letters of Recommendation – Guaranteed!

There are Five Primary Factors Required to Gain Admission to Oxbridge and other Elite Prestigious Russell Group Colleges and Universities:

1. The Highest Attainment at A-level and Pre-University Academic Achievement Grades

2. The Rigor of the Senior Secondary High School or Sixth Form attended.

3. A Winning Personal Statement Essay.

4. The Best Letters of Recommendation – Expert Testimony.

5. Several Elite Prestigious Colleges and Universities also require an in-Person Interview.

The Interview is at the heart of Oxbridge and several other Russell Group Admissions.

How students should go about the business of obtaining the Best Letters of Recommendation/Expert Testimony:

1. Ask your Three Top Senior School O-Level and Sixth Form A-Level Teachers. Three Top Professors for Undergraduates applying to Graduate Programs. The Teachers/Professors selected to write your winning letters of recommendation should be those whom you're impressed upon with your academic scholarship and other gifts and talents.

2. Ask two of the Teachers/Professors to each write a letter supporting your applications to the list of various Oxbridge Colleges

and other prestigious Russell Group Colleges and Universities, or USA Ivy League, and 18 other elite prestigious colleges and universities. Tell your Teachers/Professors why the letters are so important to your aspirations and career goals. Tell each Educator why you chose them to support your applications. The higher the rank of the teacher/professor, such as Chair of Department, Academic Dean/Head of Studies, or Principal, the more weight is given to the letter of recommendation by the Admissions Selection Committee at your desired higher education institutions. Indeed, of all your other teachers/professors whom you could choose to do the honor, you're intentionally placing your Referees in high regard and trust. Make certain to tell each of them that you've discussed the matter and your rationale for your referee choices with your parents.

3. The Secondary Factors of the Admission Application include but are not limited to aspects like extra-curricular – Leadership Ability such as Speech and Debate, Arts – Music and Drama, Sports, Legacy Alumni - Parents and other Family/Relatives, and Demographics – for Diversity among the Student Body. Obtain our USA version of this guidebook, on Admissions to Independent Elite Boarding & Day Schools and Ivy League & Stanford and MIT in the United States of America.

There are two additional Primary Factors in the Admission Applications Process for Students applying to Graduate School or Professional School.

1. The two Research Papers/Academic Writing Samples – the higher education institutions are interested in your ability to write and conduct independent research at the Graduate level. Submit your two best pieces of written work that have been evaluated by your Teachers/Professors.

2. Resume/Curriculum Vita – the higher education institutions are interested in knowing how you made good use of your time during summer vacation periods during your Undergraduate years – such as Study abroad, Internships, and the like. Make an appointment with your Guidance Counselor and or your College/University Careers Officer to help you with creating and developing a winning resume.

Bonus: Ace the Interview! Get Your Ivy League and or other Elite Prestigious College and University Offer!

Start doing your research the moment you decide to apply to a college or university that requires an interview as part of the application for admission. Prepare for possible questions you might be asked and how to respond, demonstrating your intelligence.

Think of who you are now and who you desire to become in your future career.

Think of what you have accomplished already and what you desire to accomplish in the future.

Think of a time when you and your family and your teachers were proud of your achievements.

Think of where you are now, where you desire to attend college/university, and where you desire to practice your career.

Think why you're a high achiever, why you desire your intended higher education Course of Study, and why you're applying to particular colleges and universities.

Think about how you've achieved your current level of success and how your desired colleges and universities will help you to develop and sustain your future success.

Get to know as much as you can about your desired college/university in general and in particular about the research interests/publications of the Academic Scholars in your department of chosen Course of Study – major and minor concentrations. What do you want to learn and gain from admission to study at your top chosen college/university?

There's no greater cardinal sin than applicants who show up for an interview without any serious prior knowledge of the institution in general and, worst yet, of the research interests of the Academics in their chosen intended field of study. Please do not make this common mistake. Go on the websites of the colleges and universities and learn as much as you can about the Professors – their Publications – learn their titles and preview their peer reviewed Scholarly Journal Articles and their book chapters and books they're authored and co-authored.

Demonstrate with your responses how your research interests align with the work of the department via mentioning publication works of current Academics in the department as well as Emeritus Academics. Mention the publications of other Academics in other comparatively elite prestigious colleges and universities whose research is similar and with whom some of the Academics you're interviewing may have co-authored and published. This presents you as highly intelligent, as you regard persons with similar research interests to your own; thus, you do not appear to simply only trying to impress the Academics with whom you're currently interviewing but rather showing that you have wider knowledge of your research interests with knowledge of the leading scholars in your chosen field/subject of study. This also implies that you're interested in Graduate School studies, developing within your chosen field with their guidance. They will want to choose you before you have an opportunity to interview with the Academics in the other colleges and universities you're mentioned. Academics like students who're applying not only for the 'name' of the college/university but that the decision to apply is also based in part on the Scholars who will be engaged in your teaching and learning development as you advance and make progress towards your chosen career. This will set you apart, putting your application in contention as a serious candidate for admission to your top choice college/university.

A Final Note on the Admissions Process

Admissions Officers compare students' Standardized Test scores, as well as the Academic Rigor of the schools attended by the applicant's seeking admission to elite prestigious institutions. Their decisions to grant Admission are often based on 'The Like Me Syndrome' - applicants most similar to their own educational backgrounds. Who are the Admissions Officers at Oxbridge and Ivy League? They are most often Alumni of Oxbridge and St. Andrews, and other Elite Prestigious Russell Group Colleges and Universities, Ivy League and Stanford and MIT, and other elite prestigious colleges and universities in the UK and US. Hence, Admissions Officers consciously or unconsciously admit/make offers to more than half the incoming Freshers Class each year, to applicants with proximity to their own personal educational experiences. This preference is known as 'Signaling' – choosing applicants from the Power Elite – known as Prestige Schools. This crosses over into every aspect of social organization and culture with regard to education and employment (London's Financial District, Downing Street and Westminster – Parliament and the Supreme Court, are filled with Oxbridge and St. Andrews and Russell Group Graduates), and in the US the same is true of Ivy League and Stanford and MIT graduates, and in every Country in our World prestige schools and colleges and universities reign supreme. Admissions Officers are 'People with Power,' and people with power are beholden to other 'People with Power.' Membership to the Power Elite starts with Membership at highly selective World Renown Boarding Prestige Schools in the UK, USA, and Switzerland. The Golden Ticket to Membership to Oxbridge and St. Andrews, and other elite prestigious Russell Group Colleges and Universities in the UK, Ivy League and Stanford and MIT in the US, and other elite prestigious colleges/universities. The most prestigious Secret Societies of our World.

The Prudence of our Platinum Individualized Consulting Service can help your family navigate the process of choosing the right school for your children. Please complete the General Inquiry Form on the Contact Page of our website. If you would like to be considered for reduced consulting fees, please also complete the application through FACTS: https://online.factsmgt.com/signin/4M3CT

The assessment report we receive from FACTS will help us in determining the amount of your fee remission consulting fees for each child and/or tutoring fees for each child. All Boarding Schools in the United Kingdom offer fee remission bursaries in varying amounts; some Senior Public Boarding Schools offer scholarships in varying amounts. Some universities in the UK, including Oxbridge Colleges and Academic Departments, offer some scholarships in varying amounts. UK Residents pay the Local Authority Rate – Home Fees, and EU Citizens also pay the same rate as UK Residents. Overseas – non-EU residents pay a higher rate. There are scholarships for non-EU students to help afford the overseas fees, such as the Overseas Research Student Scholarship known as the ORS which reduces the overseas students' rate to the UK Home/EU Rate. Also, the most prestigious scholarship - the Rhodes Scholarship to Oxford, the Clarendon Scholarship at Oxford, and like the Rhodes - the Gates Scholarship to Cambridge. US Students can also apply for the Fulbright Scholarship, the Marshall Scholarship, your local Rotary Club and more. Ask the departments at the schools, colleges, and universities and academic departments where you're applying for a list of scholarships with details on how to apply for those scholarships. Please do not let the ability to pay discourage you from choosing to apply for the best educational opportunities.

We look forward to reviewing your children's application/s for Platinum Consulting Services. We receive many more applications than we can accept; however, we endeavor to select the students with the most academic promise for success at Boarding Schools, Oxbridge and St. Andrews, and other elite, prestigious Russell Group Colleges and Universities. In the event that you're offered a spot with one of our Senior Platinum Consultants, we look forward to guiding you and your children through this enrichment process.

In the event that we are over-subscribed and are without any available Platinum Consulting spots, we recommend that you consider A Telethon Consultation Appointment with our President to steer you in the right direction of boarding school and college or university choice. Indeed, it is amazing how much knowledge on this process you can acquire and gain in a 10-minute conversation. Please note that our President specializes in Platinum Consulting in the following areas: Admissions to Oxbridge and elite prestigious Russell Group Colleges and Universities, Admissions to Boarding Schools UK & USA & Switzerland, General Ivy League Admissions Knowledge and Process, in particular Ivy League Non Traditional/Alternative Admissions Process, such as Adult Continuing Education for Bachelors and Master's Degrees in Evening and Online Programs at Ivy League and other elite prestigious colleges and universities.

We hope that parents and students alike find this guidebook easy to read and a good resource for selecting the best local Primary Independent Day Schools in your Local Education Authority, the best Preparatory Boarding Schools, Senior Secondary Public Boarding High Schools, and Pre-College Programs, to prepare for entry to your ultimate Oxbridge and St. Andrews and other elite prestigious Russell Group colleges and universities to prepare to ace Undergraduate and 26 subsequently Graduate and Professional Schools. Also, for those wishing to study abroad (obtain our guidebook on Admissions to Independent Elite Boarding & Day Schools and Ivy League & Stanford and MIT in the United States of America. The Golden Ticket to Ivy League and other Elite prestigious Colleges and Universities in the USA - membership to the prestigious secret societies of our World.

We wish you the very best with all your endeavors from Reception/Kindergarten, Preparatory Junior School, to Senior Secondary School, to Sixth Form College, Undergraduate, Graduate and Professional Studies, and in your chosen career/s. In the event that parents and students would like additional assistance in selecting the best Day Schools, Boarding Schools, and Summer Programs in the UK, US, and Switzerland, please complete the General Inquiry Form on the Contact Page of our website: http://www.boardingschoolsivyleagueoxbridge.com

Remember: All schools and all grades are not considered equal. Schools and Grades are stratified – based on the type of educational institution and the faculty assigning the grades to students' assignments/work products.

We look forward to serving your family.

Thank you for helping us help you raise your game.

Every good wish and many thanks for choosing:

http://www.boardingschoolsivyleagueoxbridge.com

Recommended Reading

The Cloistered Elite: *A Sociological Analysis of the English Public Boarding School.*

Five Centuries after this publication, the same schools in the UK have a significant number of students each year matriculating at Oxbridge and St. Andrews and other elite prestigious Russell Group Colleges and Universities. Independent/Private Boarding Schools in England are referred to as Public Schools. They're called Public – simply because they're open to receiving applications from the general public – students from all socioeconomic backgrounds can apply. Schools operated by Local Governmental Education Authorities – are referred to as State Schools.

Times Higher Education Supplement.

Provides insight into the rankings and League Tables of Preparatory Schools/Junior Boarding Schools, Senior Secondary Boarding High Schools, Oxbridge and St Andrews and other elite Russell Group Colleges and Universities in the UK, as well as International Rankings of Boarding Schools, Colleges, and Universities.

Annual Calendar/Weekly Planner

September

1	2	3	4	5	6	7
8	9	10	11	12	13	14
15	16	17	18	19	20	21
22	23	24	25	26	27	28
29	30					

September
First Week

Second Week

September
Third Week

Fourth Week

October

1	2	3	4	5	6	7
8	9	10	11	12	13	14
15	16	17	18	19	20	21
22	23	24	25	26	27	28
29	30	31				

October
First Week

Second Week

October
Third Week

Fourth Week

November

1	2	3	4	5	6	7
8	9	10	11	12	13	14
15	16	17	18	19	20	21
22	23	24	25	26	27	28
29	30					

November
First Week

Second Week

November
Third Week

Fourth Week

December

1	2	3	4	5	6	7
8	9	10	11	12	13	14
15	16	17	18	19	20	21
22	23	24	25	26	27	28
29	30	31				

December

First Week

Second Week

December

Third Week

Fourth Week

January

1	2	3	4	5	6	7
8	9	10	11	12	13	14
15	16	17	18	19	20	21
22	23	24	25	26	27	28
29	30	31				

January
First Week

Second Week

January
Third Week

Fourth Week

February

1	2	3	4	5	6	7
8	9	10	11	12	13	14
15	16	17	18	19	20	21
22	23	24	25	26	27	28
29						

February
First Week

Second Week

February
Third Week

Fourth Week

March

1	2	3	4	5	6	7
8	9	10	11	12	13	14
15	16	17	18	19	20	21
22	23	24	25	26	27	28
29	30	31				

March
First Week

Second Week

March
Third Week

Fourth Week

April

1	2	3	4	5	6	7
8	9	10	11	12	13	14
15	16	17	18	19	20	21
22	23	24	25	26	27	28
29	30					

April
First Week

Second Week

April
Third Week

Fourth Week

May

1	2	3	4	5	6	7
8	9	10	11	12	13	14
15	16	17	18	19	20	21
22	23	24	25	26	27	28
29	30	31				

May
First Week

Second Week

May
Third Week

Fourth Week

June

1	2	3	4	5	6	7
8	9	10	11	12	13	14
15	16	17	18	19	20	21
22	23	24	25	26	27	28
29	30					

June

First Week

Second Week

June
Third Week

Fourth Week

July

1	2	3	4	5	6	7
8	9	10	11	12	13	14
15	16	17	18	19	20	21
22	23	24	25	26	27	28
29	30	31				

July
First Week

Second Week

July

Third Week

Fourth Week

August

1	2	3	4	5	6	7
8	9	10	11	12	13	14
15	16	17	18	19	20	21
22	23	24	25	26	27	28
29	30	31				

August
First Week

Second Week

August
Third Week

Fourth Week

www.ingramcontent.com/pod-product-compliance
Lightning Source LLC
Chambersburg PA
CBHW041149110526
44590CB00027B/4176